LET'S TRAVEL TO HAWAII

Hawaii Travel Guide for Kids

Created by
Lori Biswell and Gina Garippo

Let's Travel to Hawaii-Hawaii Travel Guide for Kids

ISBN: 979-8-9953338-0-7

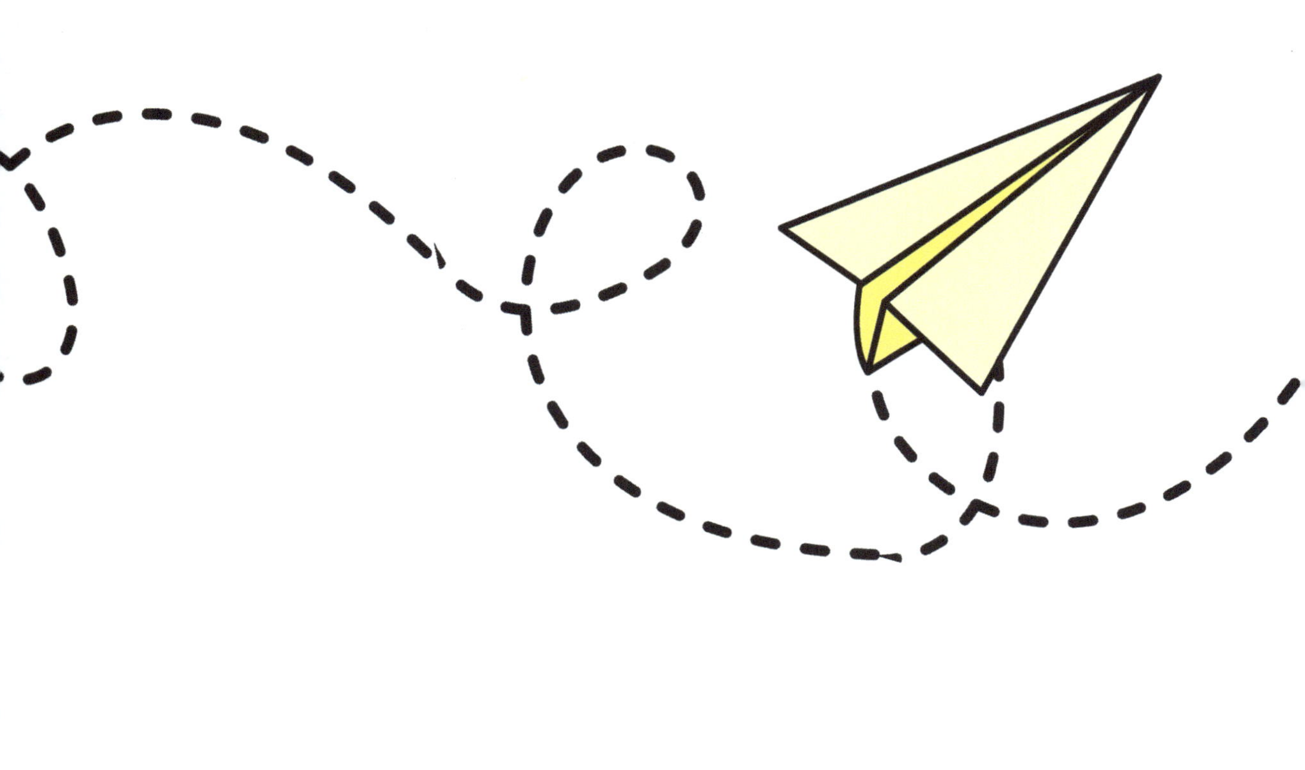

Where in the

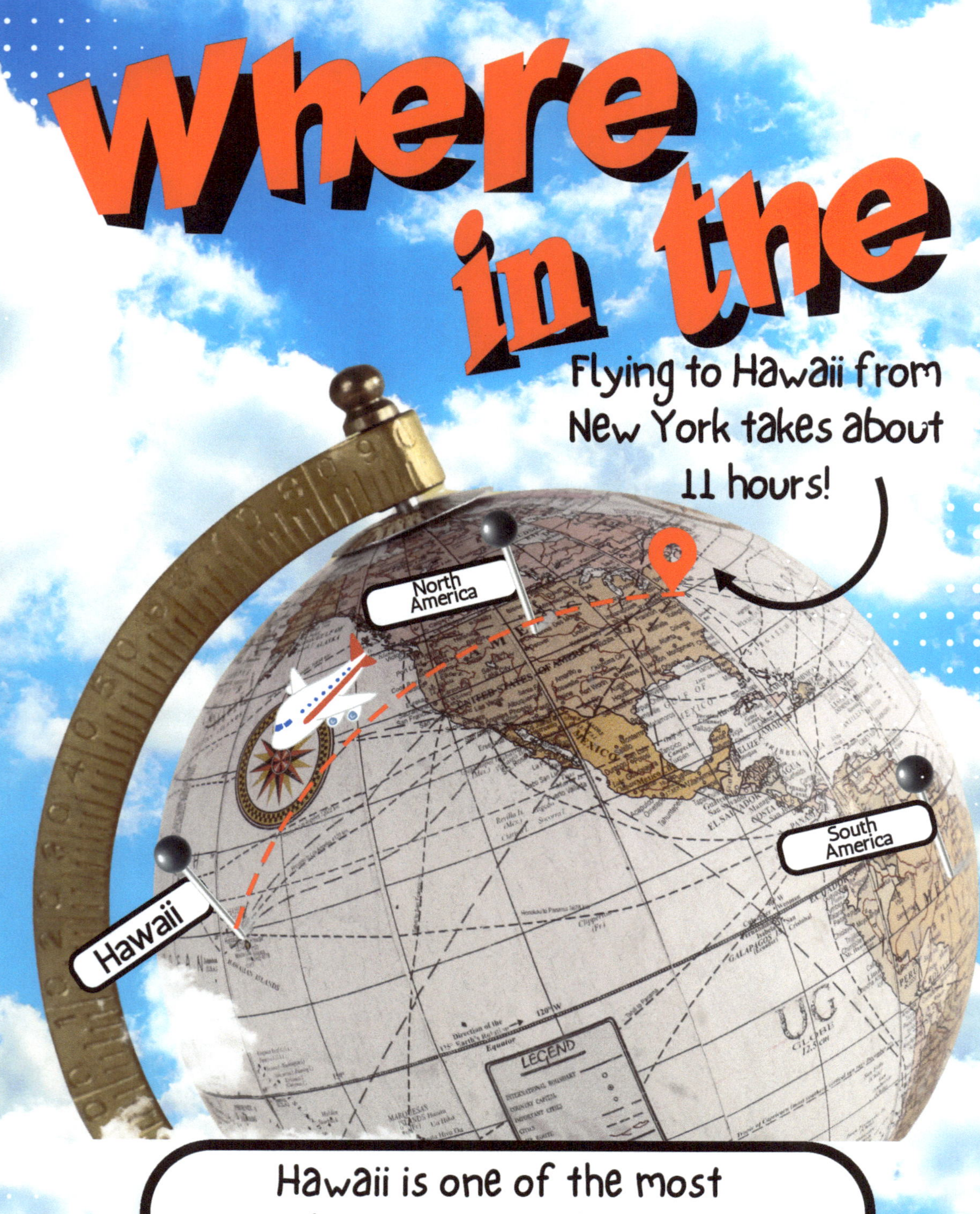

Hawaii is one of the most isolated places on Earth. Even though it's far from anywhere else, people all over the world know about Hawaii's beautiful islands and rich culture.

World?

Hawaii sits in the middle of the Pacific Ocean

Did You Know?

Hawaii is actually made up of 137 islands! Besides eight main islands, there are 129 smaller islands too. (People don't live on most of them though.) These islands stretch over 1,500 miles of ocean. That's like traveling from Austin, Texas all the way to New York City!

If you dug a hole straight through the Earth from Hawaii, you'd pop out in southern Africa!

Hawaiian Islands

Hawaii is not just one island, but a string of islands! these islands were formed from volcanos deep under the sea.

As the Hawaiian islands age, they are worn away by wind and waves. Take a look at the difference in their size! The Big Island of Hawaii is the newest island and Niihau is the oldest.

1

The Hawaiian islands are far out in the Pacific Ocean because of a **hot spot**–a super hot place deep inside the Earth where melted rock, called magma, pushes upward. When magma breaks through the ocean floor, it's called lava.

2

Layer by layer lava piles up on the ocean floor above the hot spot, forming an underwater volcano. When it grows tall enough to rise above the water, an island is born!

3

Once each Hawaiian island formed, it didn't just stay put! Deep under the island, a huge moving tectonic plate called the Pacific Plate carried it away from the hot spot–just like a giant conveyor belt. Then a new island started forming in its place.

That's why there isn't just one Hawaiian island, but many!

VOLCANOES

The same hot spot deep in the Earth that created the Hawaiian Islands is still pushing melted rock to the surface today. That means if an island is over the hot spot, its volcanoes can keep spilling lava, which slowly builds new land!

KABOOM!

Not all eruptions explode! Many ooze and spread lava like hot syrup.

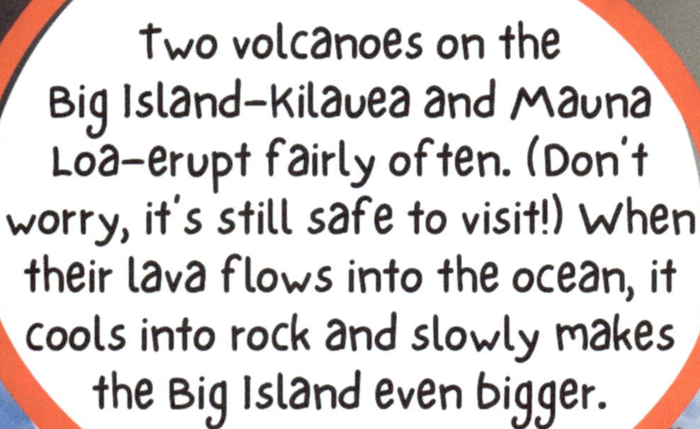

Two volcanoes on the Big Island—Kilauea and Mauna Loa—erupt fairly often. (Don't worry, it's still safe to visit!) When their lava flows into the ocean, it cools into rock and slowly makes the Big Island even bigger.

BAM!

The hot spot that's helping the Big Island grow is also building a brand-new volcano deep under the ocean called Loihi. One day, it may become a new Hawaiian island! Don't pack your bags yet though. Scientists think it will take at least 10,000 years before Loihi finally pops above the waves.

Mauna Kea, a dormant volcano on the Big Island, is the tallest mountain on Earth! Although we can only see part of it, Mauna Kea is over 32,000 feet tall from it base deep under the sea. That's taller than Mount Everest!

Kilauea

An extinct volcano is done for good. It's not expected to erupt again. A dormant volcano is just resting—it could wake up and erupt one day!

GROWN IN HAWAII

SUGARCANE

Sugar comes from the tall stalks of a plant called sugarcane. Polynesians brought sugarcane to Hawaii more than 1,000 years ago. It wasn't just a sweet treat—people also used it for all sorts of things, even as medicine!

For many years, sugarcane and pineapple were two of Hawaii's biggest crops. Yum! People came from Japan, China, the Philippines, Portugal, and other countries to work on the plantations. their hard work helped shape Hawaii's culture today.

Hawaii's last big sugar plantation closed in 2016 —but sugar is still an important part of the islands' story.

Hawaii is a sweet place to visit!

Macadamia Nuts
Macadamia trees grow...macadamia nuts! People sometimes call them "mac nuts" for short.
these trees originally came from Australia. In Hawaii, they were first planted to block the wind for other crops, but farmers discovered they were delicious! Soon, they started planting lots of them.
With their super tough shells, macadamia nuts are some of the hardest nuts to crack!
COFFEE
Although coffee hasn't always been grown in Hawaii, it's now a big deal! Coffee is one of Hawaii's most important crops today. Next time you're at the grocery store, look for Kona coffee! It comes from Hawaii's Big Island and is world famous.
Cut open a papaya and you'll see pinkish-orange fruit with shiny black seeds in the middle. It tastes a little like a cantaloupe. Besides growing on farms, papaya trees grow in many family gardens too! In Hawaii, papayas are a favorite fruit, especially for breakfast.
PAPAYA

NOW SHOWING... EARLY HAWAII!

People from all the islands of Polynesia are called Polynesians. that means Hawaiians are Polynesians too!

King Kamehameha was also known as Kamehameha the Great!
The first people sailed to Hawaii from other Polynesian islands more than 1,000 years ago. Each Hawaiian island had its own chief, its own rules, and its own way of doing things.
In 1810, Kamehameha became the very first king of Hawaii! He united all the islands into one kingdom. He also worked to protect Hawaiian culture and traditions as visitors from other countries began arriving.
After the islands were united under one king, Hawaii became a thriving kingdom. Years later, the monarchy was overthrown, and the United States took control of the islands. In 1959, Hawaii became the 50th state—and through it all, the Hawaiian people remained strong.

I ♥ HAWAII
FUN
Hawaiian Flag
There are no billboards in Hawaii! The state banned them to protect the natural beauty.
What?
WITH ITS BEAUTIFUL BEACHES, COOL VOLCANOS, AMAZING HISTORY, UNIQUE CULTURE, YUMMY FOOD, AND FRIENDLY PEOPLE - THERE'S NO PLACE LIKE HAWAII!
HAWAII
POSTAGE
TWO CENTS
The state capital is Honolulu, which is on the island of Oahu.
INTERNATIONAL
AIRLINES
HONOLULU
36-18-75
Hawaii is nicknamed "the Aloha State" for its aloha spirit—a deep respect and love for each other.
HAWAI'I
USA 44
Aloha

Hawaii is the only state made up of just islands and the only one outside of North America. It's also the only state that was once ruled by royalty!

Do you live in another U.S. state (not counting Alaska)? Here's a fun tip! When you leave Hawaii, don't say you're going back to the United States...you're already there! Instead, say you are headed to the mainland—that's what people call the 48 connected states.

State Flower

Yellow Hibiscus

DID YOU KNOW

Hawaii became the 50th U.S. state (the last one!) in 1959.

BEST DAY EVER!

NOT EVERYONE WHO LIVES IN HAWAII ARE CALLED HAWAIIANS. THAT SPECIAL NAME IS JUST FOR PEOPLE WHOSE FAMILIES HAVE NATIVE HAWAIIAN ROOTS. OTHERS WHO HAVE LIVED IN HAWAII FOR A LONG TIME ARE CALLED LOCALS.

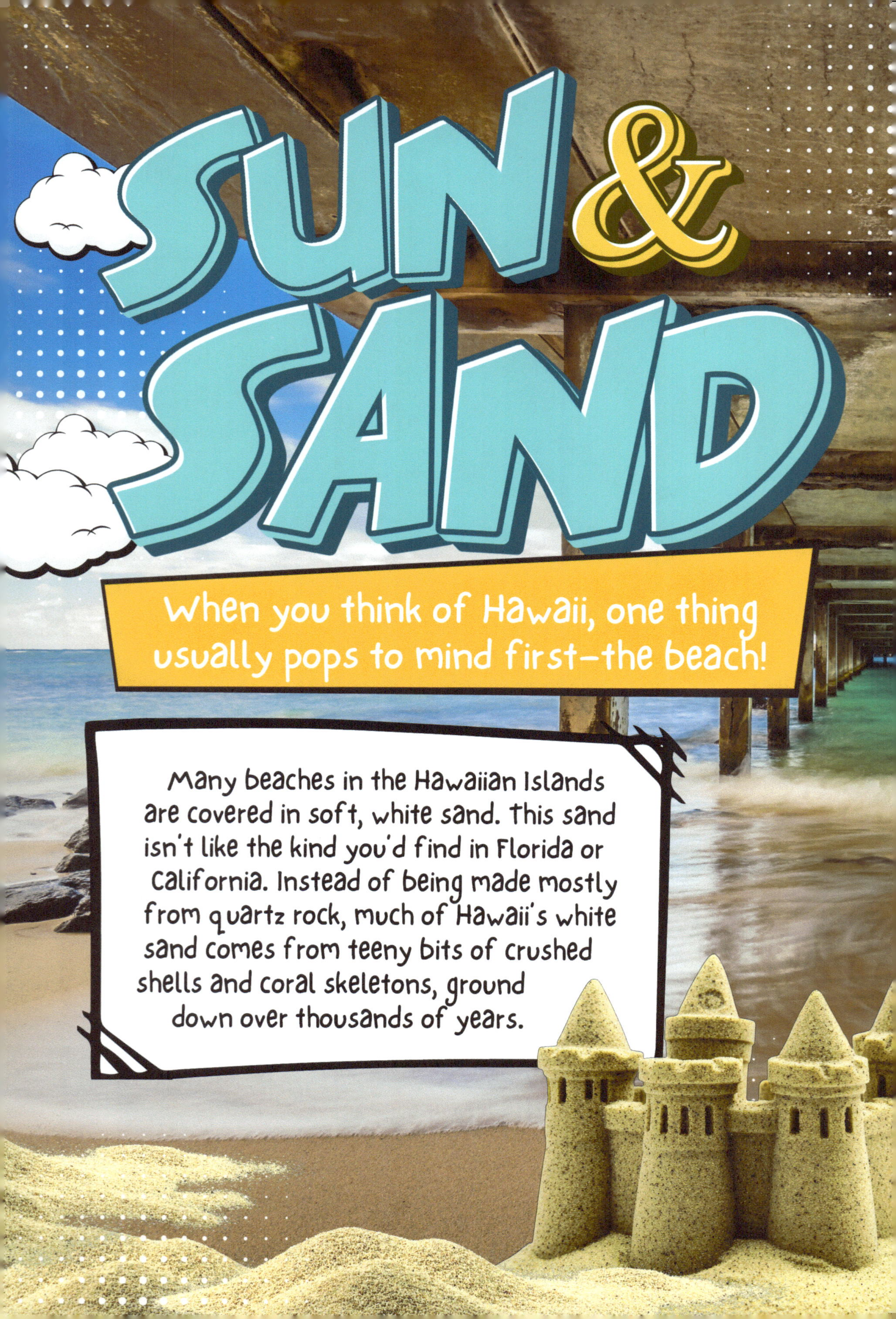

SUN & SAND

When you think of Hawaii, one thing usually pops to mind first—the beach!

Many beaches in the Hawaiian Islands are covered in soft, white sand. This sand isn't like the kind you'd find in Florida or California. Instead of being made mostly from quartz rock, much of Hawaii's white sand comes from teeny bits of crushed shells and coral skeletons, ground down over thousands of years.

Think Hawaii's beaches are just white? Think again! Some beaches have black sand, made from lava that flowed into the ocean, cooled, and then broke into tiny pieces. This lava contains a mineral called magnetite that can make some black sand magnetic! Other beaches have red sand from iron-rich volcanic rock or even green sand made from a crystal called olivine, found in certain Hawaiian lava.

Green sand beaches are so rare there are only a few in the whole world!

It's against the law to take sand, rocks, or coral from Hawaii!!

DID YOU KNOW?

Parrotfish love to munch on the algae that grows on dead coral. When they do, they swallow tiny bits of coral along with it. These fish grind up the coral with their strong teeth—and later, poop out sand! One large parrotfish can make over 2,000 pounds of sand in a year. Talk about a beach factory!

SHARK ATTACK!
About 40 different kinds of sharks are found in Hawaii!
WHAT?
Hawaii's Most Extreme Sharks!
Biggest Shark: Whale Shark (bigger than a school bus, but eats only tiny plankton!)
Smallest Shark: Pygmy Shark (about the size of a banana)
Fastest Shark: Shortfin Mako (swims up to 45 miles per hour)
Most Powerful Bite: Tiger Shark (due to large jaw muscles & saw-like teeth)
Deepest: Sixgill Shark (lives thousands of feet below the surface)

Sharks have lots of rows of teeth. When one tooth falls out, a new one slides right in! Some species lose more than 50,000 teeth in their lifetime!

CALL THE TOOTH FAIRY!

ARE SHARKS DANGEROUS?

Breathe easy, shark bites in Hawaii are super rare! Most sharks around the islands are small, shy, and spend most of their time in deep water. Even sharks that swim near the shore rarely cause problems. that's because sharks aren't interested in people as food (whew!). they prefer tasty fish and other sea creatures.

BOOM!

You are more likely to be struck by lightning than get bitten by a shark!

Sharks are super sneaky hunters! One reason? They have an amazing power called electroreception!

Tiny pores on their heads let them sense faint electric signals from other animals when they move. that's why hammerhead sharks sweep their heads side to side over the ocean floor, like a fish detector! And when sharks get close, fish freeze and hold their breath.

WOULDN'T YOU?!

Totally WEIRD & WACKY
HAWAIIAN SEA CREATURES
These creatures can't move on their own. They float in the ocean and drift with the wind and currents. Stay clear if you spot them—they pack a powerful sting.
Portuguese Man o' War
YIKES!
Dumbo Octopus
These rare animals all have one funny feature—big fins that look like the ears of Disney's Dumbo the Elephant! They live deep in the ocean and flap their fins to glide through the dark water.

Hawaiian Monk Seal
these endangered animals are the only seal native to Hawaii. they spend most of their time in the warm water. When they're on land, they move around by wiggling on their belly!
Hawaiian Green Sea Turtles
these gentle sea turtles can grow very large and may live to 100 years old! Look for them swimming near the shoreline. In Hawaii, these turtles are called honu and often seen as symbols of good luck.
Long-Spined Sea Urchin
these dark black creatures look like a ball with pointy spines. they're cool to look at but be careful. Getting stung can really hurt! If you go snorkeling, you might spot some hiding in the rocks.
WOW!

SO MUCH TO SEE

Hawaii is full of colorful fish!
How many can you find?

UNDER THE SEA
Yellow tang
Moorish Idol
Reef triggerfish
this is Hawaii's
official state fish!
Parrotfish
In Hawaiian,
the reef triggerfish is called
humuhumunukunukuapua'a.
Try to say that three times fast!

A WHALE'S TALE

Whale watching is super fun! It's exciting to see a whale's tail–also called its flukes–pop out of the water when diving. Sometimes you might even see a whale breach! This is when it uses its fins to throw itself up and out of the water.

WOW! A humpback whale is as heavy as 8 elephants!! Imagine it crashing back into the ocean!

NOTCH

LEFT FLUKE

RIGHT FLUKE

Did You KNOW?

Researchers can recognize individual whales by looking closely at their flukes. Just like your fingerprints, flukes have unique markings that make each one special. No two flukes are exactly the same!

If you see a whale in the ocean, it might even have a name! Scientists give specific whales their very own name to help study and track them.

Every winter, humpback whales travel to the warm waters of Hawaii to find a mate and have babies. these huge creatures swim here all the way from Alaska, where they spend the summer eating and growing strong. that's an epic 3,000-mile trip!

Are we there yet?

WHEW!

Sing-a-long ANYONE?

Male humpback whales are known for their amazing singing in oceans all over the world! Every winter in Hawaii, these giant whales sing the same song over and over again. Sometimes, whales join in together—almost like a choir! their songs can last a few minutes or go on for hours. Whales thousands of miles apart may sing the very same tune!

How do whales decide which song to sing? Nobody knows for sure! We do know that whales are creative—they add their own sounds or changes to a song. Sometimes these changes catch on and are picked up by other whales, making the tune more and more complex. Every few years, they switch to a brand-new song!

Flowers of

Hawaii is bursting with natural beauty! Besides sunny beaches and blue waters, there are plants and flowers everywhere. Can you believe over 1,000 kinds of plants are native to Hawaii? That means they arrived all on their own, traveling by ocean waves, birds, or even the wind! Other plants and flowers were brought by people from faraway places, but now are part of what makes Hawaii so special.

Ma'o Hau Hele (Hawaiian Hibiscus)

This bright yellow hibiscus with a deep red center is Hawaii's state flower! There are six other types of hibiscus that are native to Hawaii too. They have many different colors—from white and pinkish-purple to vibrant red.

Bird of Paradise

This exotic flower was brought to Hawaii from South Africa. Today, it grows in parks and gardens all over the islands. Bird of Paradise is cool because it looks just like a bright, tropical bird hiding in the grass!

HAWAII

Pua Kala (Hawaiian Poppy)

This large white flower has a bright yellow center and prickly green leaves. Look fast—the blooms last only one day! Thankfully, new flowers pop open all the time. The native plant spreads easily and is super tough. It can even survive fire!

Apocynaceae (Plumeria)

The plumeria flower is not native to Hawaii, but it might be one of the first flowers you see here! That's because this sweet-smelling flower is often used to make leis. Plumerias grow so well in Hawaii because they love the tropical climate and don't mind the wind and salty air.

Nanu (Hawaiian Gardenia)

This white flower, which grows on small trees with dark glossy leaves, smells a little like coconuts! Nanu used to grow all over Hawaii but is now endangered. It's only found on a handful of islands.

In Hawaii, wearing a flower behind your ear is pretty—and can also tell a story. It's said that a flower over your right ear means you're single. A flower on your left ear means your heart is taken. Today, many people just wear flowers because they look and smell beautiful!

SO PRETTY!

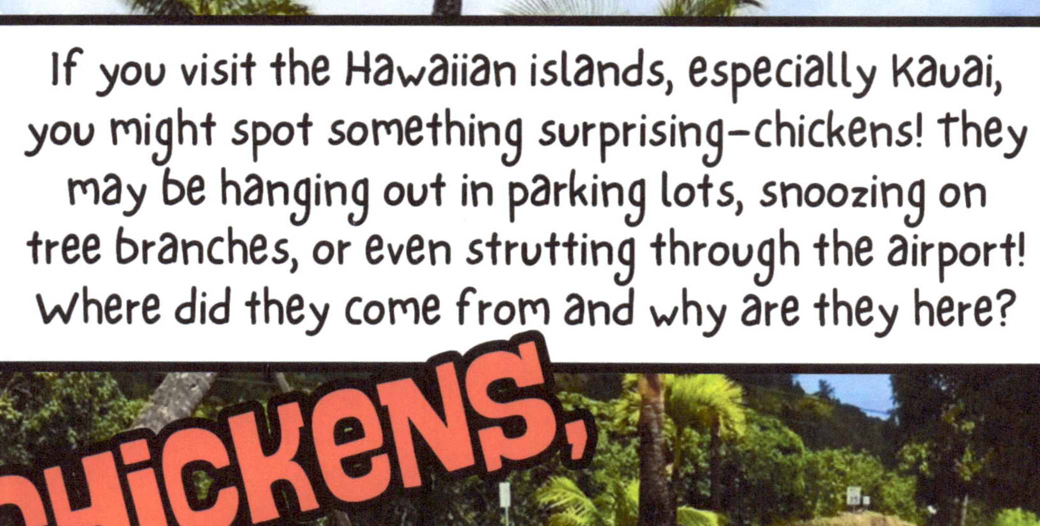

CHICKENS, CHICKENS EVERYWHERE!

With no coyotes, foxes, or snakes around, Hawaii's wild chickens are mostly free to wander!

Do local people eat wild chickens? Most of the time, no! These chickens are pretty lean and their meat can be tough.

the chickens you see on the streets of Kauai and other islands come from a mix of different birds. A long time ago, Polynesians brought chickens to Hawaii. these birds came from a wild chicken called the red junglefowl. Later, people from Europe brought farm chickens too. Over time, these two kinds of birds mixed. the result? the noisy wild chickens you see roaming around the islands today.

On Kauai, many farm chickens escaped into the wild when hurricanes blew in a few decades ago.

hen

rooster

the super colorful boy chickens are called roosters. their feathers are bright orange and deep red. the girl chickens, called hens, are dressed in light brown feathers so they can hide more easily.

Wild chickens in Hawaii sleep in trees! Since they are part red Junglefowl, it's in their blood! Trees also give them shelter, food, and a safe spot away from cats and dogs.

DID YOU KNOW?

HAWAIIAN NIGHT SKY

Take a look at the night sky in Hawaii...it's Magical! Because the islands are far away from big cities, the sky gets super dark. This makes it awesome for stargazing!

A long time ago, people sailed across the huge Pacific Ocean without GPS! They used the stars to navigate! They also watched the clouds, wave patterns, and even birds to find their way.

How?

Check out those stars!

See if you can find these constellations in Hawaii's night sky.

TAURUS

Taurus looks like a bull's head with big horns! If you visit Hawaii in winter, you might spot it. That's the only time it shows up here!

SOUTHERN CROSS

Hawaii is the best place in the United States to see the entire Southern Cross. Look for it low in the southern sky! Years ago, Hawaiian navigators used these stars to help them find south while sailing across the ocean.

PLEIADES

This tiny cluster of twinkling stars is called Makali`i in Hawaiian, which means "little eyes". In late fall, it appears in the evening sky. Its return marked the beginning of Makahiki–a special season that reminded people to give thanks for the year's crops.

SCORPIUS

Have you seen Disney's Moana? In the movie, Maui carries a magical fishhook. Based on Hawaiian legend, the group of stars we call Scorpius is said to look like Maui's fishhook! Stories say Maui used his hook to pull the islands up from the ocean floor.

PEGASUS

Some people see Pegasus as a flying horse. In Hawaii, the same stars are sometimes seen as a kite. Hawaiian navigators used stars like these to guide their canoes, and storytellers used them to teach lessons about chiefs, the land, and the ocean.

Hawaiian Words

You'll hear English spoken all over Hawaii–but did you know the islands also have their own beautiful language? It's more than just words. It tells the story of how Hawaiian people are connected to each other and nature. Learning a few Hawaiian words can mean a lot to people in Hawaii. Want to give it a try?

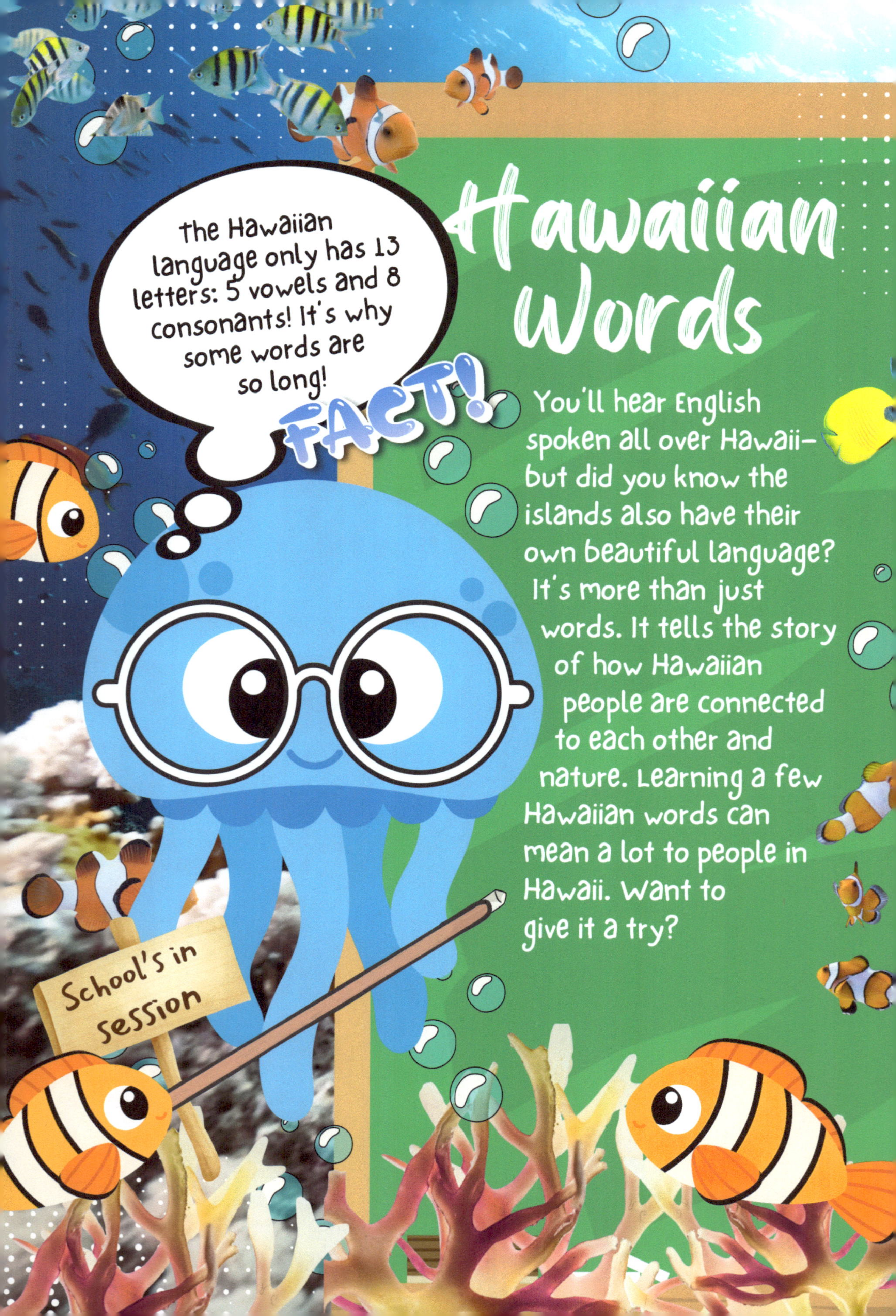

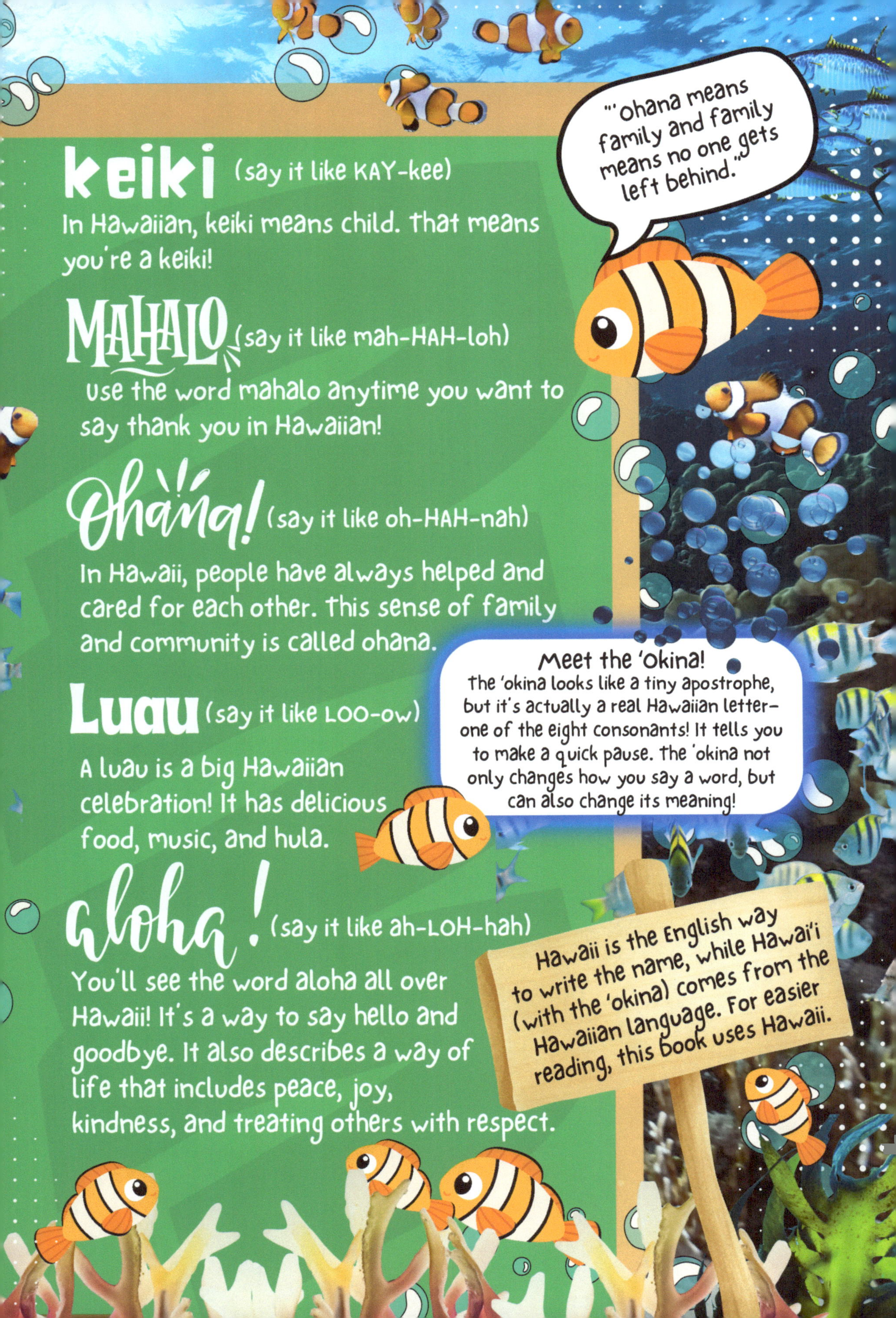

keiki (say it like KAY-kee)

In Hawaiian, keiki means child. That means you're a keiki!

MAHALO (say it like mah-HAH-loh)

Use the word mahalo anytime you want to say thank you in Hawaiian!

Ohana! (say it like oh-HAH-nah)

In Hawaii, people have always helped and cared for each other. This sense of family and community is called ohana.

Luau (say it like LOO-ow)

A luau is a big Hawaiian celebration! It has delicious food, music, and hula.

aloha! (say it like ah-LOH-hah)

You'll see the word aloha all over Hawaii! It's a way to say hello and goodbye. It also describes a way of life that includes peace, joy, kindness, and treating others with respect.

ART

Hawaii is filled with amazing artwork! Beyond colorful paintings, handmade jewelry, and beautiful photos, you can admire art all over the islands—sometimes in the most unexpected places! Here are just a few:

In Hawaii, traditional wooden carvings called ki`i were created to represent gods, ancestors, or spirits. Today, you may see tiki-style carvings in souvenir shops, but traditional ki`i are meaningful cultural artworks created by skilled carvers.

Hawaiian Ki`i Carvings

Many artists have made their home in Hawaii. Can you think of a better place to create?

You may have been given a lei at your hotel or visit to a luau. Did you ever think about it as a piece of art? the flowers, shells, nuts, and feathers on a lei aren't just strung together–they're carefully arranged into a beautiful, wearable creation!

Leis

Surfboards aren't just for riding the waves–they can be awesome works of art too! traditional Hawaiian surfboards were carved from trees. today, many artists paint surfboards with designs inspired by island life. You can spot these colorful surfboards all around the islands.

Surfboards

Did You Know?

Much of the art in Hawaii is inspired by nature–from hibiscus and plumeria flowers to sea turtles and volcanoes.

Petroglyphs

Hundreds of years ago, early Hawaiian people carved images into lava rocks. these pictures–which include canoes, turtles, people, and more–give us a glimpse into their everyday life. You can still see some of these ancient petroglyphs on the islands today!

MUSIC

The music of Hawaii is a mix of sounds from many people and places! Polynesians came across the ocean to the islands with chants, rhythms, and drums. Later, people from Portugal brought the ukulele–a small instrument that became a big part of Hawaiian music.

Today, you can hear all kinds of music in Hawaii, from rock and jazz to a special kind of reggae. Each one celebrates the spirit and traditions of the islands!

UKULELE

The ukulele isn't just a fun instrument–it's part of Hawaii's heart and soul! In the 1800s, even Hawaiian kings and queens played it at parties and special events.

The ukulele looks like a little guitar but has a sound all its own. There are four sizes of ukuleles, and each has a different tone. No matter the size, the ukulele has a happy sound that may remind you of the islands.

Ukulele means "jumping flea." Some people say it got its name because your fingers hop quickly across the strings when you play!

Percussion instruments—like drums—have been part of Hawaiian music for hundreds of years. they were used with chants and hula to tell stories or celebrate important events.

Drums help create the strong, steady rhythms of Hawaiian music. the pahu and ipu are especially important:

Many traditional Hawaiian instruments are made from things found in nature—like gourds, bamboo, stones, and even sharkskin!

DRUMS

Pahu (say PAH-hoo) is a very special Hawaiian drum made from the trunk of a coconut tree, with sharkskin stretched across the top. Long ago, it was considered sacred and traditionally played by very important people during ceremonies and rituals.

IPU

Ipu (say EE-poo) is a traditional Hawaiian drum made from a hollow gourd. It's often used in hula to help keep the beat.

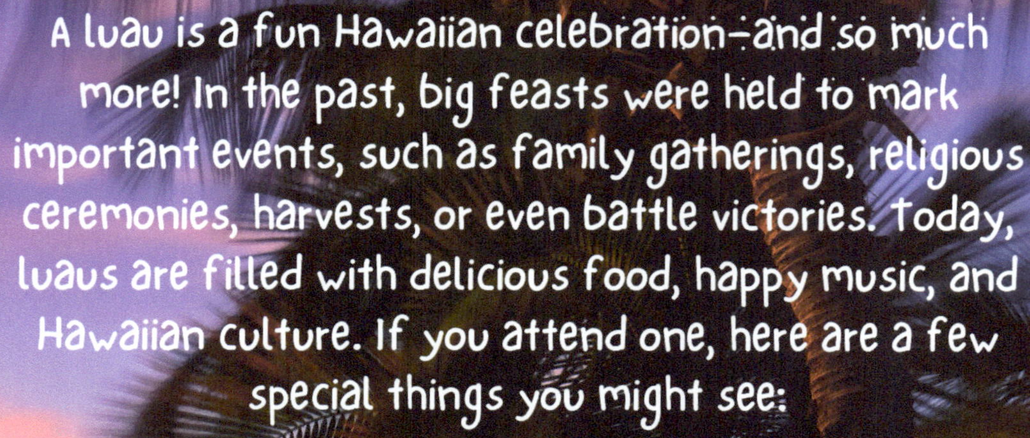

A luau is a fun Hawaiian celebration—and so much more! In the past, big feasts were held to mark important events, such as family gatherings, religious ceremonies, harvests, or even battle victories. Today, luaus are filled with delicious food, happy music, and Hawaiian culture. If you attend one, here are a few special things you might see:

Lei

When you go to a luau, you might be welcomed with a beautiful lei! It's a necklace made of flowers, leaves, or nuts—and it's a super special gift. A lei is a symbol of friendship and respect.

Going to a Hawaiian Luau?

Hula

You've probably heard of hula dancing—but there's a lot more to it than you might think! Every movement the dancer makes has a special meaning. Hula is performed to chants, drums, or songs, and together the movement and music tell a story. Traditionally, hula was used to share history, teach lessons, and even pray.

Feast

POI

The food at a luau is really tasty! You might get to try kalua pork, fish, chicken, sweet potatoes, and tropical fruit. Don't forget to look for poi! It's a purple-colored food that looks like a smooth, sticky paste. It's made from the taro plant and has been eaten in Hawaii for hundreds of years!

Conch Shell

The conch shell, called a pū in Hawaiian, is more than just a beautiful shell. It can also be used to send a message! When blown in just the right way, it makes a long, deep sound that can travel far. The pū is often sounded at the start of a luau or to announce special events like weddings or festivals.

LUNCH TIME!

Are burgers and fries your go-to? Don't worry, Hawaii has all your favorites! But while you're here, try a few local foods too.

From Polynesian voyagers to families from Asia and other parts of the world, Hawaii is home to all kinds of people—and all kinds of food! A fun way to try these tasty dishes is at a food truck.

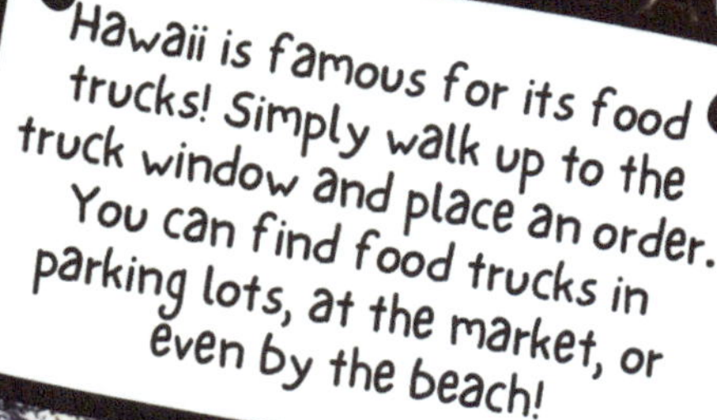

Hawaii is famous for its food trucks! Simply walk up to the truck window and place an order. You can find food trucks in parking lots, at the market, or even by the beach!

POKE

Poke' (rhymes with okay) is usually made with raw tuna —yep, it's super fresh! the seafood is mixed with tasty spices and sauce and then served on its own or over rice.

HULI HULI CHICKEN

This is a yummy kind of grilled chicken. Its coating gets sweet and sticky as it's turned on the grill. Huli means "turn" in Hawaiian.

KALUA PORK

This tender, shredded pork is cooked in a special way! A whole pig is wrapped in banana leaves and roasted over hot rocks in an underground oven called an imu.

SPAM

Spam is a type of processed meat that comes in can. It was used during World War II to feed soldiers but is still popular in Hawaii today. Even McDonald's in Hawaii sells it for breakfast!

Shave ice looks a lot like a snow cone—but it's not the same thing! Snow cones are made with crunchy, crushed ice. Shave ice is made by shaving a big block of ice into fine, fluffy flakes before pouring syrup on top. These flakes soak up all the flavor which makes it super yummy!

YUM!

In Hawaii, this tasty treat is called SHAVE ice (not shaved ice)!

Workers from Japan brought shave ice to Hawaii more than 100 years ago!

You can make your shave ice super fun by adding tasty extras. Try it with a snow cap (that's sweet milk drizzled on top) or ice cream in the center. You can also add sweet beans, fresh fruit, or chewy mochi balls (made of Japanese rice cakes).

Want to try **Tiger's Blood??** This shave ice flavor is made with strawberry, watermelon, and coconut syrup. While the name sounds scary, it's delicious!

TODAY'S FLAVORS

Cherry
Coconut
Cotton Candy
Green Apple
Mango
Orange
Pineapple
Strawberry
Watermelon

WHICH WOULD YOU CHOOSE?

GO NUTS for Coconuts!
the coconut is not actually a nut—it's a fruit!
Coconuts are super cool because every part of the fruit can be used for something. Nothing goes to waste!

The Husk

...is the hairy stuff on the outside of the coconut. It's used for gardening and can be made into things like doormats and ropes.

The Shell

...is the tough outside part of the coconut. It can be polished up to make bowls and decorations. It's even used to make charcoal!

The Meat

...is the fluffy white part inside the coconut. You can munch on it as a snack or bake it into tasty treats. It's also used to make coconut oil and coconut milk.

The Liquid

...inside is coconut water. You can drink it straight from the coconut! It's super hydrating and packed with electrolytes. Think of it as nature's sports drink.

Coconuts float and don't soak up water so they can travel far across the ocean on their own. When washed up on a beach, they can grow into brand new trees!

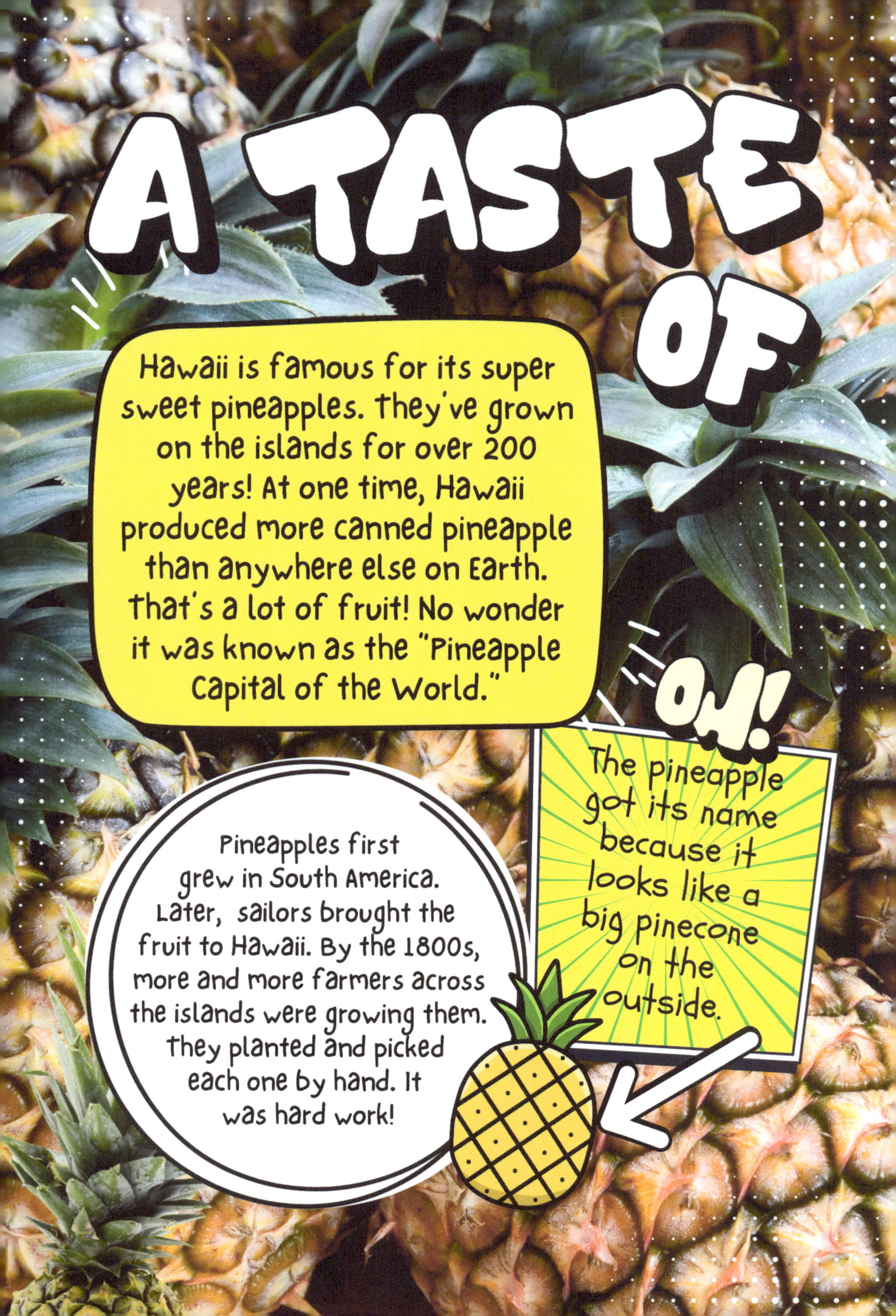
A TASTE OF
Hawaii is famous for its super sweet pineapples. They've grown on the islands for over 200 years! At one time, Hawaii produced more canned pineapple than anywhere else on Earth. That's a lot of fruit! No wonder it was known as the "Pineapple Capital of the World."
OH!
The pineapple got its name because it looks like a big pinecone on the outside.
Pineapples first grew in South America. Later, sailors brought the fruit to Hawaii. By the 1800s, more and more farmers across the islands were growing them. They planted and picked each one by hand. It was hard work!

PARADISE

Today, you can visit the famous Dole Plantation on Oahu. Its Pineapple Garden Maze is super fun! Put on your gym shoes—it has more than 3 miles of paths!

In 1901, James Dole started the Hawaiian Pineapple Company out of his barn on Oahu. He helped make canned pineapple popular all around the world. The company grew fast and became the biggest producer of canned pineapple anywhere. He later bought most of the island of Lanai and turned it into a huge pineapple plantation.

SURF'S UP!
Surfing is a huge part of Hawaii's history and culture. It began in ancient Polynesia, but Hawaii helped turn it into the world-famous sport it is today. That's why Hawaii is often called the birthplace of modern surfing!
Surfers love the shaka sign! In Hawaii, it stands for friendship, good vibes, and the Aloha spirit. Many people call it the "hang loose" sign!
ALOHA!

Surfboards come in all kinds of sizes. Longboards—similar to the very first surfboards—are up to 10 feet long and super stable on the water. Shortboards are smaller, faster, and better for experienced surfers who want to do cool tricks.
HMMM
Early surfboards were carved from heavy wood. Now, they're lighter and float better too!
In early Hawaiian culture, surfing wasn't just for fun. It was part of traditions and ceremonies. At one time, certain surf spots and special boards were reserved for chiefs and royalty. Riding the waves showed their power, skill, and bravery.

SURF SCHOOL!

Want to be a grom
(a kid who surfs)?
Learn these rad surfing terms!

Hang ten

When a surfer wraps all 10 toes over the front of the board

Ankle Biters

Tiny waves that barely reach your ankles

Wave Hog

Surfer who catches a lot of waves and doesn't share them

Barrel

When a wave curves over, forming a tunnel of water a surfer can ride inside

Line-up

Area in the water where surfers wait for waves

SURFER'S DREAM!

Want to catch a wave? Surfing takes strong arms for paddling, good balance, and just the right timing to pop up on your board. It's really fun to practice! The best part? Almost anyone can be a surfer—from a total beginner (you have to start somewhere!) to an Olympic athlete.
COOL
Oahu's North Shore is famous for surfing! Winter waves there can reach more than 30 feet—that's as tall as three basketball hoops stacked on top of each other! It's an awesome place to watch pro surfers ride the giant waves.
OH!
Hawaii has tons of surfing schools where you can learn how to ride your very first wave!

Hawaiian LEGENDS

Have you ever been on the edge of your seat listening to an amazing story? Imagine sitting under the bright Hawaiian sky long ago, listening to the waves crash nearby as a storyteller begins...

The people of Hawaii have been sharing powerful stories and legends for thousands of years. These tales were passed down from generation to generation—long before books or written language existed in Hawaii!

Many of these exciting stories are about gods, goddesses, heroes, and villains. They tell how the Hawaiian Islands were formed, describe how people lived long ago, and share lessons about history, culture, and values.

There are many gods and goddesses in traditional Hawaiian stories. Every part of nature—from animals to waves—was associated with a god or goddess. Here are a few you might hear about:

Laka—goddess of Hula and Forest Growth

The graceful swaying of a hula dancer is said to be inspired by Laka, goddess of hula. Her spirit is also thought to move through the flowing leaves of the forest.

Kāne—god of Life, Fresh Water, and Sunlight

Think about rain falling on the mountains and streams sparkling in the sunlight—Kāne, god of life, is linked to water, creation, and every living thing around us!

Kanaloa—god of the Ocean

Picture the sparkling blue ocean full of turtles, fish, and rolling waves—Kanaloa, god of the ocean, is said to watch over the sea and all the creatures in it.

Pele—goddess of Fire and Volcanoes

Imagine glowing lava running down a volcano—Pele, the goddess of volcanoes, is said to live in the crater of Kilauea!

BEWARE!

Pele's Curse

One popular Hawaiian legend says that taking lava rocks or sand from the islands can upset Pele, the goddess of volcanoes. People believe this can bring bad luck! Even today, tourists who have taken rocks often mail them back to Hawaii to end their troubles.

SUNSETS

Every evening in Hawaii, something magical happens–the sunset!! Head out to the beach or find a spot with a clear view and take in the special show!

Why are sunsets in Hawaii so **AMAZING?**
Lots of reasons!
Hawaii's tropical location, salty ocean breeze, gentle winds, and volcanic dust all combine to create brilliant sunsets with intense colors. Plus, because Hawaii is in the middle of the ocean, you often get a wide, open view of the horizon. It's like a painting! Watch it glow with the deep reds, pinks, and oranges.

Tips for Taking Awesome Sunset Pictures:

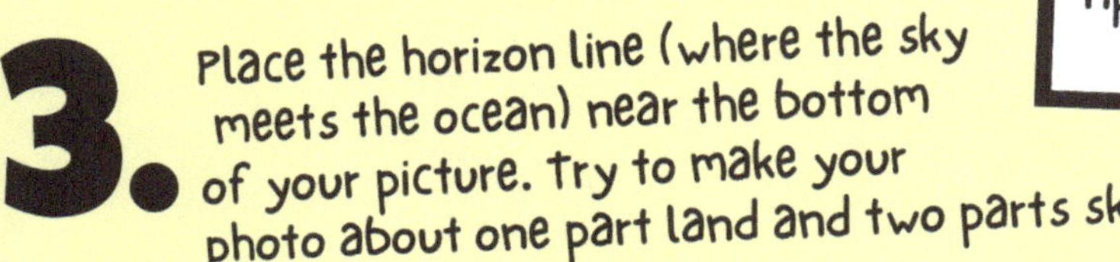

1. Make sure the flash is off to capture the stunning natural light.

2. Turn your phone or camera sideways to take a wide picture. This way, you can include more of the landscape—like trees, mountains, or the beach—which makes your sunset photo extra pretty.

3. Place the horizon line (where the sky meets the ocean) near the bottom of your picture. Try to make your photo about one part land and two parts sky.

4. Have fun trying out different filters! Pick one that makes the colors pop—like the "vivid" setting.

5. Include cool stuff into your photo to make it unique. Try capturing the branch of a nearby palm tree, someone walking on the beach, or an interesting cloud in the sky.

Have you heard of the green flash? When conditions are just right you can sometimes see a tiny flash of bright green at the moment the sun dips below the ocean. Watch closely as the sun disappears. If you're lucky, you might catch the magic!

SEE YOU ON OUR NEXT ADVENTURE!

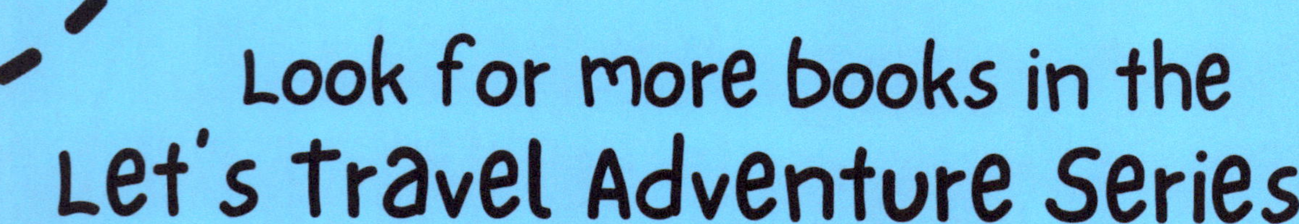

Look for more books in the Let's Travel Adventure Series

Where should we travel next?

www.ingramcontent.com/pod-product-compliance
Lightning Source LLC
LaVergne TN
LVHW071155160826
845679LV00003B/663
* 9 7 9 8 9 9 5 3 3 3 8 0 7 *